Original title:
The Sea's Gentle Whisper

Copyright © 2025 Creative Arts Management OÜ
All rights reserved.

Author: Robert Ashford
ISBN HARDBACK: 978-1-80587-426-3
ISBN PAPERBACK: 978-1-80587-896-4

Whispers of the Blue Horizon

Tall tales told by waves so loud,
Fish wear fins and swim in a crowd.
Seagulls gossip about beach ball fights,
While sandcastles reign as kings of heights.

The tide beckons with a playful grin,
As crabs do the cha-cha, a dance to win.
Jellyfish joke with a wobbly sway,
Silly sea turtles join in the fray.

Gentle Rhythms of Water

Bubbles giggle as they pop and burst,
While starfish endure a slow, funny first.
An octopus waves with all of its arms,
Declaring itself the king of charms.

Seashells whisper secrets to the sand,
About a clam who had a rock band.
The tide taps its toes, keeping the beat,
As dolphins dance and wiggle their feet.

Secrets of the Rolling Surf

Waves roll in, sharing jokes from afar,
A shrimp with a mustache claims to be a star.
Crabs crack jokes, each one a little shy,
While seaweed sways, almost passing by.

A clam sings loudly, though it's off-key,
Decorated with pearls, it's quite a sight to see.
Each splash tells a story, a giggle here and there,
As laughter floats softly upon the warm air.

Hushed Conversations of Sand and Surf

Grains of sand share tales, oh so light,
About the waves sneaking off in the night.
A crab with a joke and a pinch of humor,
Says, "Why don't fish play cards? They might get a rumor!"

The moon grins down, a playful delight,
As shadows of dolphins leap into sight.
Together they laugh, the shore's merry crew,
Winking at the stars, oh so bright and blue!

Symphony of Salt and Light

The ocean sings a tune quite strange,
With fish that dance and waves that range.
A seagull drops a nut on shore,
As crabs all scuttle, looking for more.

The sunbeams twinkle like a clown,
While dolphins jump and spin around.
A sea turtle winks, oh what a sight,
Making seaweed hats, just for delight.

The Quiet Call of Distant Horizons

The tide whispers tales of pies and cake,
Of jellyfish doing the ocean break.
A starfish plays the ukulele there,
While shells gossip, tossing salty air.

The waves sometimes laugh with a bubbling cheer,
As plankton throw a party, oh dear!
The dolphins are jesters, full of glee,
In the underwater circus, as grand as can be.

Soft Echoes of Nautical Nights

Moonlight dances on the rippling waves,
While crabs wear hats, it's the latest craze.
Starfish form a band, they play all night,
Their rock and roll brings the fish delight.

The octopus juggles pearls for fun,
And the sea cucumbers join in on the run.
Mermaids giggle, showing off a flip,
As the turtles trade jokes on their evening trip.

Whispers of the Deep Blue

Bubbles rise like tiny balloons,
As fish throw a party, blasting tunes.
Anemones sway, looking so spry,
While shrimp in tuxedos strut by.

The underwater world is a playful spree,
With whales cracking jokes, how funny they be!
Even the coral joins in the jest,
In this splashy world, they all are the best.

Tranquil Tide's Sigh

The ocean's hum, a friendly tease,
It tickles toes and sways the knees.
A hermit crab scuttles with glee,
Saying, "Who knew shells were for free?"

Dolphins frolic in silly loops,
While seagulls plot like feathered stoops.
They steal your fries, oh what a crime!
A beach day laughing all the time!

Lull of the Coastal Whisper

A soft breeze chats, so light and clear,
It whispers jokes for all to hear.
The tide retreats with a chuckle low,
"Who'd leave their sandcastles to go?"

A crab declares, "I'm king of the beach!"
While starfish claim they're out of reach.
But every wave just rolls and grins,
As everyone knows, it always wins!

Shadows Dance on Serene Waters

The shadows prance like silly mates,
As fish play tag, oh what great states!
A clam does cartwheels, quite absurd,
"I don't do pearls, I dance," it purred.

Jellyfish float with a wobbly sway,
They giggle softly, "Let's dance today!"
"Who brought the music?" a dolphin asks,
"It's just the splash of our playful tasks!"

Tracing the Shoreline's Secrets

Footprints sketch tales of toe-tapping fun,
A beach ball rolls, oh we want to run!
The sand tickles toes with every glide,
As waves wander in on a joyous ride.

A pelican lands with a loud thud,
"Mistook my splash for a diving flood!"
The shoreline giggles, secrets to share,
"Let's dip our toes in without a care!"

Murmurs Beneath the Waves

Bubbles rise up with a pop,
As fish wear frocks and start to bop.
Crabs dance like they're in a show,
While seagulls caw, 'Look at my toe!'

Starfish giggle, they can't stop,
Sandy flounders do a flip-flop.
Octopuses trade silly hats,
While turtles laugh and hug the mats.

Clams tell tales of tides and swells,
As jellyfish wave, 'Come hear our bells!'
A conch shell sings a funky beat,
That's how we groove on the ocean street!

Dive into joy, don't be a grump,
Life's too short to miss this jump.
Underwater raves, every day,
Join the fun, just swim and sway.

Serenity's Embrace

In the calm where seagulls tease,
The starry sky drinks in the breeze.
With little crabs in stylish wear,
They scuttle off without a care.

Sunbathers sporting quirky hats,
Chasing shadows, avoiding chats.
Waves crash softly, then retreat,
They leave behind a shell-shaped seat.

Dolphins leap with silly grace,
Greet the sun, start a race.
Mermaids giggle with their tails,
As the wind tells all their tales.

Laughter floats like bubbles high,
Beneath the waves, the fish all sigh.
Life is fab in this harbor's light,
Just bring your joy, it feels so right!

Ocean's Soft Serenade

A clam hums notes while brushing sand,
The breeze whispers, 'It's all quite grand!'
Surfboards giggle with a wave,
As salty snacks the seagulls crave.

Waves snooze softly, taking breaks,
While crabs make friends and share their flakes.
Starfish lounge, reclining wide,
With sunglasses on, they bask with pride.

Seashells chat with funny rhymes,
Such silly stories, broken times.
The sand's a stage for all to see,
Just join the fun, come laugh with me.

Watermelons float in the tide,
While dolphins ride with bubbly pride.
When sunset giggles, bringing cheer,
We toast to joy, our hearts sincere!

Tidal Dreams Unfurled

Tides come in with a playful cheer,
While otters surf, oh dear, oh dear!
They tumble, fall, then stand up straight,
In this wet world, there's no debate!

Barnacles sing on old boats' hulls,
While barn owls plot their daring pulls.
A fish pulls a prank on a crab,
Who opens wide, then flips and grabs.

Seashells spinning, what a sight,
They twirl and whirl, then take flight.
Kites in the sky, fish on a loom,
Dance under stars and the glow of the moon.

A whale cracks jokes, everyone roars,
With laughter echoing on sandy shores.
As tides recede, we wink and play,
In the luscious echo of a wave-filled day.

Fluttering Hearts Along the Coast

Seagulls squawk like gossip queens,
Chasing crabs through sandy scenes.
A conch shell holds the latest news,
While starfish dance in joyous shoes.

Waves send messages with frothy grins,
Tickling toes as laughter spins.
Each splash a punchline, a wave's embrace,
As shells play hide and seek in the race.

A beach ball rolls with a silly bounce,
While toddlers run, their joy profound.
Dunking heads, the brave ones boast,
While flip-flops fly – oh, what a coast!

The tide brings jokes, like mermaid tales,
While seashells whisper giggly wails.
With every swell, a chuckle bursts,
Life's quirks unfold, like ocean's thirst.

The Ocean's Gentle Caress

Salty breezes tease the ear,
Jellyfish float, yet not a fear.
Crabby friends wave pincers high,
While dolphins surf and laugh on by.

A surfboard slips, a surfer flops,
In endless waves that bubble and pop.
The fish are busy, doing a jig,
While octopuses put on a big gig.

Seashells giggle under the foam,
They'll protect dreams, like a cozy home.
Each splash a joke from the ocean floor,
With sandcastles built to adore.

Anemones dance in bright array,
While tide pools host a crab ballet.
Life's fishy tales keep laughter alive,
On this shore, where wonders thrive.

Silence Beneath the Surface

Bubbles rise like secrets shared,
Fish in tuxedos, all prepared.
The seaweed sways like it knows the tune,
While turtles perform a slow cartoon.

An octopus pulls a funny face,
As sea cucumbers wriggle with grace.
Beneath the waves, a comedy show,
Where little shrimp steal the limelight glow.

Clownfish hide in coral caves,
Cracking jokes while the ocean waves.
A whale sings softly, a lullaby,
As jellyfish giggle and float on by.

With every splash, a punchline flows,
Where silence whispers, laughter grows.
Submerged in joy, beneath the blue,
The ocean's humor shines right through.

Graceful Currents in a Whisper

Currents twirl like dancers light,
As sea snails race, what a sight!
Starfish salute in their slow parade,
While fish have fun, new jokes are made.

The tide draws near, like an eager friend,
Sharing secrets it will lend.
With each crest, a chuckle breaks,
The ocean's humor - that's what it takes.

Seashell ears listen, filled with glee,
To the tales of crab and little flea.
Anglerfish grins with a wily glance,
Inviting all to join in a dance.

Waves leap high with splashes bright,
As laughter ripples in golden light.
In every deep and every bend,
The water sings, and laughter's friend.

Beyond the Turbulent Surface

Waves that giggle, splash and play,
They dance around in a silly way.
Seagulls cackle, wearing a grin,
As they dive in, it's chaos to win.

Bubbles burp, a merry tune,
While crabs scuttle, taking a swoon.
Octopus juggling, quite a sight,
In this watery realm, all feels light.

Fish parade in sequined scales,
Telling tales of windy gales.
Their laughter rides the foam so high,
As dolphins leap and touch the sky.

With every crest, a chuckle near,
The ocean's giggles we can hear.
Making splashes, what a sight,
A jolly journey from day to night.

Chants of the Ocean's Heart

Whales sing songs, so loud and clear,
While clowns in wetsuits draw us near.
Starfish waltz with silky grace,
In this waterlogged, wild space.

Crabby poets, scribbling in sand,
With every wave, they take a stand.
Their rhymes are funny, filled with cheer,
Making us laugh as they come near.

Lobsters laugh with twinkling eyes,
While sea turtles wear silly ties.
They hold a feast, with fish galore,
Who knew the ocean was such a bore?

So let's dive deep, and take a peek,
Where funny fish all try to speak.
Embrace the jest in salty air,
For the ocean's heart is fun, I swear!

Caressing the Undercurrents

Gentle tides tickle toes with glee,
While seaweed twirls, wild and free.
The current pulls, a playful tease,
As fish play tag beneath the seas.

Eels are dancing, full of flair,
While shells gossip without a care.
Crabs in costumes steal the show,
In underwater cabarets, they flow.

Mollusks cheer with every sway,
As dolphins join the frothy play.
They whirl and twirl, skip and glide,
In the deep blue, where jokes abide.

So if you're down for a funny quest,
Join the party beneath the zest.
In hidden depths where laughs abound,
The currents' joy is easily found!

Echoes at Daybreak

Morning light brings jokes anew,
Shells chuckle softly as they do.
Crabs in pajamas, stretching wide,
With sleepy laughs on the ocean's ride.

The sun peeks in, a glowing grin,
While flat fish giggle, "Let's begin!"
The tide rolls in, a wavy tease,
With clams that shuffle, aiming to please.

Sea otters snicker, floating there,
Tossing seaweed without a care.
They tumble, play, then stop and stare,
At all the fun that's in the air.

So with each wave, join the cheer,
For morning's mirth is ever near.
Where echoes lift and spirits rise,
Each daybreak brings sweet surprise.

Dreams Adrift in the Water's Glide

Chasing waves on a floatie,
Sipping dreams served in tea.
Fishes laugh at my splashes,
As they swap jokes with the sea.

Seagulls dive, looking for snacks,
They stole my sandwich in flight.
I wave goodbye to my lunch box,
With a giggle that feels just right.

Crabs form a conga line dance,
Scuttling sideways in glee.
They've got moves that make me laugh,
Feeling jealous of their spree.

Under the sun, we all frolic,
Mermaids join in, oh what fun!
We play tag with a big old whale,
Ending the day with a pun!

Fluid Whispers of the Night

Moonbeams slither on water,
Mermaids sing silly tunes.
Octopuses juggle seaweed,
Underneath the glowing moons.

Starfish wear hats made of shells,
A crab serves popcorn with flair.
Laughter dances in the air,
As jellyfish float without care.

A dolphin tells bad dad jokes,
Flipping and flopping in style.
His punchlines make all fish giggle,
Even the whales crack a smile.

The tides giggle with the breeze,
As night wraps us in a hug.
Ebbing waves whisper their dreams,
While I sleep safe in their snug.

Beneath the Feathered Skies

Kites soar like fish in the air,
Birds chirp tunes with a twist.
I wore my hat like a pirate,
As the gulls all laughed and hissed.

Pigeons land with shifty eyes,
Looking for crumbs, oh so sly.
I threw a chip; they went wild,
Chasing it with a flurry of fly.

The shoreline plays hide and seek,
As crabs sneak around in their shells.
They plot silly little pranks,
Like giving clams funny bells.

Underneath clouds made of fluff,
We gather for a sandcastle treat.
The ocean aids our grand plans,
While the tide rolls back on its feet.

Echoing Shelters of the Shore

Shells echo tales from long ago,
Echoes of laughter weave and twine.
Seagulls laugh at my flip-flops,
As I trip while searching for signs.

A hermit crab moves in slow-mo,
Trotting with style, oh so bright.
He throws a party with seaweed,
Inviting everyone in sight.

Fish gossip about the weather,
"Rain or shine, we're still the best!"
An old turtle tells his secrets,
In a shell-shaped cozy nest.

Bubbles rise with giggle fits,
Caught in coral's painted glow.
In this world of salty giggles,
Joy drifts in a sunny flow.

Harmonies Beneath the Waves

Bubbles pop like jokes on the shore,
Fish giggle and swirl, always wanting more.
Starfish dance like they're in a trance,
Seaweed sways, a wiggly prance.

Crabs wear pinchers like goofy hats,
Playing tag with sneaky fats.
A dolphin sings a silly tune,
While seagulls spin, laughing at the moon.

Shells gossip like old friends at play,
Telling tales of sun and spray.
Seashells scatter, sounding the glee,
Whispers of laughter lost to the sea.

Each wave a chuckle, a splash of cheer,
As the ocean whispers, 'Come dance here!'
The tide rolls in, with a wink and a grin,
Nature's joke, let the laughter begin!

Echoes from the Briny Abyss

A fish tells tales of underwater suns,
While octopuses juggle shells for fun.
Eels slither like they're in a race,
Cracking jokes in the watery space.

Turtles rock out with their reggae beat,
While jellyfish groove, oh so sweet.
A starfish's high-five makes you chuckle,
In this ocean, who needs a buckle?

Seagulls squawk in comedic delight,
Making waves with their flighty spite.
Anemones wave, 'Come join the spree!'
Spreading giggles beneath the sea.

Mermaids laugh, tossing their hair,
Creating whirlwinds of playful affair.
Echoes travel in a giddy flow,
Funny tales in the undertow!

Caress of the Ocean's Breath

A gentle breeze teases the sand,
While fish tickle the toes in the land.
With sea cucumbers making a fuss,
And crabs in socks creating a bus.

A pelican trips on a clam's wide grin,
Hauling a catch, he can't seem to win.
Waves roll in with a roaring cheer,
While lobsters play peek-a-boo with no fear.

Seashells giggle, 'Aren't we a sight?'
As tide pools shimmer, glimmering bright.
Sea urchins chuckle, "We're bumpy, it's true!"
In this watery world of joyful revue.

The boats bob in a whimsical dance,
As dolphins leap, giving waves a chance.
With each splash, a mirthful caress,
A fishy comedy, no need to impress!

Tranquil Ripples at Dusk

Sunset spills liquid gold on the blue,
While fish throw parties, just for a few.
Mollusks gossip, whispering low,
Clams get in on the sea's nightly show.

Waves hum softly, tickling the sand,
With a twist of a fin, and a flick of a hand.
Crabs exchanging witty little jests,
With every rippling wave, laughter rests.

The horizon blushes, a comic delight,
As seagulls perform their aerial flight.
A glowfish winks, "I'm sparkle and fun,
Join us, dear humans, we'll all be one!"

With the stars winking back from above,
The ocean giggles, spreading its love.
A melodic calm in the dusky sway,
And laughter echoes till the break of day!

Silken Currents of Dusk

The tide is here with giggles loud,
Tickling toes beneath a shroud.
Seagulls swoop and steal our fries,
While fish just swim, all sleek and sly.

A crab in shades thought he was cool,
But tripped right down—a fool at pool!
The waves roll in with a splashy cheer,
Dragonflies buzz, spreading good cheer.

Shells gather secrets, gossip flow,
They laugh at sand, so rare and slow.
With every wave that splashes down,
The ocean's clap makes all hearts frown.

But wait, there's a dolphin with a grin,
He'll steal your hat, then winks and spins!
Underneath the stars, it's such a sight,
Laughter echoes, all through the night.

Whispered Secrets of the Deep

In the briny blue, fish fling a joke,
While octopuses grin, a clever cloak.
Anemones dance, with ribbons unfurled,
Who knew sea life was so swirly-whirled?

A turtle struts with stylish flair,
While starfish play a game of dare.
With bubbles rising like giggly dreams,
The ocean floor busts at the seams!

Conch shells chuckle in the salt air,
Whispers float to a dolphin's lair.
And clams are known for their cheeky snickers,
As crabs crack jokes—no need for clickers!

Laughing waves tickle sandy toes,
Even seaweed joins in on the show.
Life beneath is a strange delight,
Where every flick is a ticklish sight.

Gentle Tide's Caressing Kiss

As I skip stones, I hear them laugh,
The water's tickle is a merry staff.
Barnacles sport hats of furry green,
Imaginary ballgames they convene.

The gulls throw shade, what an audacious crew,
Stealing chips from unsuspecting you.
With sandcastles crumbling, they claim their prize,
While tiny crabs dance, oh what a surprise!

Waves wash up with a giggly sound,
Slapping sand, then spinning around.
A fish in a bowtie gives a salute,
While seals breakdance in their slick cute suit.

Oh, the humor in each salty breath,
Soft laughter echoes, not quite like death.
So let us play where smiles abound,
And find joy in the splashy ground.

Melodies of Moonlit Waters

When the moon winks, the waves start to prance,
Fish putting on their jiggly dance.
Shells hum tunes, in a jazzy beat,
While frogs croak out happy, catchy heat.

A mermaid laughs with a golden comb,
Brushing seaweed as she makes her home.
With bubbles that pop like the best of jokes,
The waves roll in, as the seagulls poke!

Silvery fish hold a song contest,
Flipping and flopping, they know they're the best!
Sandy shores fill with echoing views,
As the tide whispers odd little hues.

Every splash sings of joy and glee,
From the deep blue to the sandy sea.
So come take a dip, where laughter resides,
In the moonlit waters, where happiness glides.

Embracing the Silent Abyss

In water deep, a fish does grin,
A shark floats by, just seeking din.
Octopus, with style, does twirl around,
While crabs compete for the funniest sound.

Seaweed dances, a wavy show,
A clam snickers, 'I'm the star, you know!'
With bubbles popping like little cheer,
The ocean laughs, it's party time here!

Clownfish giggle, hiding in caves,
While seagulls swoop like comedic knaves.
The tide pulls jokes from bottomless pits,
As starfish wear socks and make silly fits.

Cradle of the Calm Waters

Down at the shore where the sandpipers play,
A turtle thinks he's the fastest today.
He races the waves, but oh what a flop,
Just splashes and flops, it's a comedy stop.

Seashells gossip, the crabs roll their eyes,
'Who's wearing those colors?' they all theorize.
A dolphin winks, with a flick of his tail,
While a sea cucumber tells the best tale.

The lighthouses wobble like they're on a spree,
Waiting for ships, but more like a bee.
They buzz and they hum, full of laughter and glee,
But boats just sail by with an 'Oh, let it be!'

Echoes of a Peaceful Shores

When waves are laughing, the gulls take flight,
A seahorse twirls, 'Isn't this right?'
With seafoam jokes and tidal pranks,
The ocean's humor spans all ranks.

A lazy starfish naps, what a scene,
Dreaming of disco, feeling like a queen.
Clams clap their shells, in a rhythmic beat,
Making the barnacles tap their feet.

The tides carry whispers both silly and bright,
As mermaids juggle pearls, what a sight!
Playing with pirates, who can't seem to jest,
The ocean's full of laughter, it's the utmost best!

Beneath the Canopy of Waves

Bubbles float by like jokes in the air,
A fish swims through, with a twirly flare.
They chatter and giggle, the coral agrees,
The sea is a jester that aims to please.

Anemones tickle, a porpoise giggles,
While sea turtles tell tales that jolt and wiggle.
In this underwater circus, fun's never late,
Where kelp lays down the mats for the great!

Down in the depths, where the antics collide,
An eel tells a joke while the lobsters hide.
With each wave that breaks, more chuckles arise,
In this watery world, laughter never dies.

Solitude in the Ocean's Embrace

Beneath the waves, a fish does dance,
With bubbles forming, it takes a chance.
A crab walks sideways, quite the sight,
Waving at seagulls, all in delight.

Hermit crabs in homes they choose,
Snailed away when they hear the blues.
In clamshells they hide with a grin,
Wishing that normal was a funnier spin.

Octopuses juggle with eight slim arms,
Causing confusion with their many charms.
They tickle the fish, then laugh a lot,
Playing sea tag in a sandy spot.

In wake of a whale, there's a big splash,
As dolphins giggle, they dart and dash.
They argue over who's got the best flip,
While jellyfish float with a graceful trip.

Secrets Carried by the Tides

There's a shell on the shore with a tale to tell,
Of crabs in tuxedos, they dance really well.
A starfish comments, "I'm quite the star!"
While plankton party like they're in a bazaar.

The seaweed sways, it's a hair salon,
As fish come in for a quick salon dawn.
"Just a trim," says the anglerfish with pride,
While sneaky eels giggle, trying to hide.

Seagulls squawk about vogue and trends,
While puffins in coats, say, "We're not friends!"
A turtle speeds by on a chaotic spree,
Wishing for land, but laughs in the sea.

With crabs on the sand playing leapfrog,
And sea cucumbers, just wallowing in fog.
The tides keep swirling, their secrets so vast,
In the world beneath, how time flies fast!

Tides of Quietude

The ocean sighs with a giggly tune,
Fish flip-flop under the shimmering moon.
A seahorse prances, in golden array,
While clowns of the deep laugh and sway.

The lobsters march in a silly parade,
With seagulls above playing serenade.
They dance on the sand, with shells as their stage,
Squeaking out songs, filled with mirth and rage.

A murmuring wave whispers to the shore,
"Life is but a goof-off, let's laugh a bit more!"
Seahorses giggle, in a watery whirl,
As bubbles come up, and pinwheel and swirl.

The tides keep rolling in whimsical stripes,
In a world of guffaws, no one ever gripes.
So, raise up your eyes, and let laughter fly,
For in the depths, joy is the reason why!

Lullabies of the Deep

A dolphin hums a lullaby sweet,
While octopuses juggle with their eight feet.
Sea turtles yawn, and drift off to dreams,
Elephants of the sea in shimmering gleams.

With twinkling stars on the surface above,
The starfish wink, feeling all the love.
"Join the sleep party, it's all super grand!"
As sea anemones twirl hand in hand.

Whales glide by, humming whale songs,
As fish dance around, like they belong.
The tide gently rocks them in peace and cheer,
With frothy waves whispering, "Don't fear."

So, when the moonlight glistens brightly,
And the ocean chuckles, oh-so-lightly,
Close your eyes and listen close,
To the bedtime tales of the sea's merry host.

Shimmers in the Twilight Tides

In twilight's glow, a crab struts proud,
With pinchers raised, he speaks aloud.
"I'm king of this sandy, slippery seat!"
But watch your toes, he's not discreet!

A dolphin jumps in the evening air,
With all his flair, he doesn't care.
"I'm here for a splash, not to be coy!"
A fishy comedy, oh what joy!

The gulls above with their raucous rhyme,
Mix up their words, it's such a crime.
"Hey, you with the sandwich, share it wide!"
Or else we'll swoop and take a ride!

As stars twinkle on the water's face,
The jellyfish waltz with flouncy grace.
"What's your dance style? A jig or a spin?"
Just don't step close, we sting from within!

Soliloquy of the Wandering Wave

Oh, what a traveler I am today,
Rolling along, I've lost my way.
I whisper to rocks, "How's life for you?"
They shrug and reply, "Still hard as a shoe!"

A pirate hat floats by, quite bold,
"Ahoy, matey!" the wave jokes, uncontrolled.
"Just lost my ship, but picked up some glee,"
"Guess I'm a tide without a decree!"

The starfish laugh as I tumble and glide,
"Oh wave, dear wave, you've got no pride!"
I splash back, "But have you seen the view?"
They chuckle, "Yeah, but we can't swim too!"

The moon looks down, gives me a wink,
"Stop being so salty, grab a drink!"
I swirl with laughter, I rise and fall,
"Here's to my journey, the best of them all!"

A Dance Beneath the Foamy Veil

Beneath the froth, a crab plays hide,
With tiny moves, he's full of pride.
"I'm a secret agent, swift and sly!"
But he's got no cover, oh my, oh my!

A starfish spins on its pointed tip,
"Watch my dance, oh join me, hip!"
"What's that, little fish? You're too shy?"
"Not too shy, just don't want to die!"

The sponges giggle, their voices sweet,
"What's a party without some heat?"
They bubble and bounce, a wiggly crew,
"Dance with us, come join the brew!"

With laughter resonating, they all sing,
The lighter my heart, the more I swing.
A conch shells wisdom, it starts to sway,
"Just enjoy each moment, come what may!"

Chants of a Distant Swell

A swell rolls in with a cheeky grin,
"Did you hear the one about the fin?"
A fish dives deep, but then he floats,
"I'm just taking a break, I hope it's not boats!"

The shells gossip like old friends at tea,
"Did you see that wave? It's too carefree!"
They giggle and clink, as tides begin,
"Here comes laughter, let the fun begin!"

Octopus paints with tentacle flair,
"Look at my mural, it's debonair!"
But watch out, folks, it rains ink for real,
"Oops! Just my way of keeping it zeal!"

Then crabs unite for an evening chat,
"Who stole my snack? Was it you or that?"
They playfully tease, it's all in jest,
In this world of laughter, they're truly blessed!

Celestial Murmurs of the Waves

A fish wore a hat, thought it quite neat,
Tried to join a band, but missed a beat.
A crab with a drum, he took a chance,
Made all the clams do an ocean dance.

A starfish tried singing, looked pretty blue,
Found out its voice wasn't quite for the crew.
The dolphin just laughed, said, "Here's a tip,"
"Stick to your day job, don't start a trip!"

With bubbles as mic, the octopus freestyled,
Said, "I'm the best!" A jellyfish smiled.
But when it came time to drop the beat,
The squids all got tangled; oh, what a feat!

As waves rolled in with a friendly cheer,
Sea creatures joined in, a laugh to hear.
As tides rolled back, in a frothy whirl,
They knew fun's a treasure of this grand world.

Secrets Swirled in Ocean Spray

A seagull swooped low, wore shades on its beak,
Snatched a hot dog, oh what a sneak!
With ketchup and mustard, the gull took flight,
Leaving behind chaos, what a tasty sight!

The barnacles grinned, huddled in a bunch,
Told fishy jokes over a clammy lunch.
"Why don't we wave?" they chuckled with glee,
"Because our hands are stuck—can't you see?"

The whale sang a tune, a bass in the chase,
It twisted its tail and started to race.
With bubbles like notes, it tried to impress,
But ended up tripping, oh what a mess!

In the salty breeze, secrets held tight,
The laughter echoed, our hearts felt light.
As currents swirled tales beneath the spray,
We joined in the fun, come what may!

Harmonics of the Still Waters

In still waters it seems, where silence reigns,
A frog in a tux likes to play chess games.
His strategy's bold, he croaks out a plan,
But loses to fish—oh, the shame of a man!

An otter, so sly, donned a monocle too,
Declared himself wise, with a philosophical view.
"Life's just a stream, full of currents and fun,"
He splashed the horizon, just soaking the sun.

With reeds as his podium, a turtle gave speech,
"We must save the pond!" it began with a screech.
The frogs all clapped, chanting out in cheer,
While fish just rolled by, appearing unclear.

Yet stillness may hide, with giggles beneath,
Secrets around every leafy sheath.
In the calm of the waters where antics can play,
We find humor that drifts with each sunny day.

Silent Songs of the Sea

A clam played the piano, keys made of shells,
Chords of the ocean, ringing like bells.
With octopus hands, it tickled the keys,
Made the dolphins chuckle, all swaying with ease.

A lobster recited a poem of pride,
About a lost boot, who took quite a ride.
The seaweed swayed gently, joining the song,
As shrimp tap-danced, singing along.

A shark in a tux, thought he looked so fly,
But stepped on a sea urchin, oh my, oh my!
He cried out in shock, but then laughed so loud,
It echoed through waters, strong and proud.

With bubbles of laughter, cruising the tide,
The ocean holds secrets; no need to hide.
From turtles to otters, all creatures agree,
The silent songs hum, filled with pure glee.

Driftwood Echoes and Moonlit Dreams

A piece of wood floats by so grand,
I wonder if it knows how to stand.
It drifts and dances without a care,
Waving at fish with a splashy flair.

Seagulls squawk, trying to chat,
The driftwood just laughs, how about that?
With a wink and a nod, it rides each wave,
Telling tall tales, oh how it misbehaves!

At night it shines under the moon's beam,
Dreaming of being part of a team.
A pirate ship, far from its goal,
But instead it's a log, taking a stroll.

Oh driftwood, you joker, floating so free,
You're the most ridiculous thing in the sea.
With your mossy cap and your barnacle tune,
You'll always be funny—my wooden buffoon!

Beneath the Quiet Blue

Bubbles giggle, fish swim with glee,
Underneath where no one can see.
A crab spins tales of life on the sand,
Stitching a quilt with his tiny hand.

The starfish is plotting a grand little show,
With a chorus of mussels, all lined up in a row.
It's hard to take seriously, such silly folk,
When one says a joke, and the other just croaks.

A jellyfish floats with a squishy grace,
But it trips on a wave, no time to erase.
It bounces back up, all wobbly and grand,
Saying, "Life's too short to just sit on land!"

In the tranquil blue, laughter prevails,
In a world full of fins and funny tales.
With each little splash, there's joy to be found,
As the ocean hums its giggly sound.

Songs of the Peaceful Tide

The tide rolls in with a playful sigh,
Tickling the toes of every passerby.
The shells are the audience, clapping away,
As the waves perform, night turns into day.

Seaweed balloons like a silly clown,
Wobbling and bobbing, it won't wear a frown.
Anemones dance, with their petal-like flair,
Who knew sea plants could put on such air?

The dolphins join in with a flip and a twist,
Splashing and laughing, they cannot resist.
They throw a party, no fish left behind,
In this underwater scene, laughter's designed.

Oh melodies of the water, so light and bright,
Sending waves of laughter into the night.
With a wink and a splash, the ocean's our guide,
In this cheerful dance of the rolling tide.

Dreamscapes Adrift in Aqua

In dreams, I float on a bubble so bold,
Carrying secrets that the squids have told.
Octopuses giggle, wearing hats made of kelp,
"Jump in, take a ride! Just don't worry about help!"

A fish wearing glasses reads under the sun,
Scribbling nonsense for a nautical pun.
His scales sparkle bright, giving divine bling,
While the sea turtles hum, making all ocean sing.

Drifting along with a purposeful jibe,
Surfing the currents, 'tis all of our tribe.
A flotilla of laughter carried by streams,
In a world so jocular, we swim in our dreams.

So here's to the waves and the whims they impart,
For every small splash carries laughter and heart.
In aqua's embrace, we all find our way,
Through dreams dipped in joy, let's frolic and play!

Soft Footprints on Salty Shores

With squishy toes we tread the sand,
Each step a print, our own made brand.
Seagulls squawk, a feathery jest,
While crabs dance sideways, a comical fest.

Waves giggle as they race and play,
Chasing our laughter as we sway.
But watch your flip-flops, don't let them flee,
Oh there they go, for the tide's a spree!

Sandy snacks, we munch with glee,
A seagull grabs one, 'Hey! That's for me!'
Yet, we can't help but chuckle and cheer,
As we dodge the splash, sipping on our beer.

So here we prance, in bright sun's glow,
With slippery feet, and hearts aglow.
Each stumble and trip, a story to tell,
On salty shores, where we laugh and dwell.

The Calm Between Storms

In the calm, the breeze starts to chuckle,
As clouds play hide-and-seek, a playful shuffle.
Fish poke their heads, curious and sly,
'Is it time for a swim?' they gigglingly cry.

A surfboard rides the gentle crest,
Wobbling like a dancer, struggling best.
Then whoops and hollers from a fellow rider,
'They said it'd be easy, they're just a liar!'

Ocean's calm is a jester's stage,
Where waves tease the boats, a daily rage.
But fish don't mind, they're simply keen,
To play tag with dolphins, the sea's silly scene.

So we sit on the shore, drink in tow,
Cracking jokes as the calm winds blow.
When storms do arrive, oh such a flurry,
We'll laugh through the chaos, no need to hurry.

Beneath the Surface's Veil

What lies below? A curious thought,
Bubbles and wiggles, some battles fought.
Anemones dance, the stars of the show,
While fish trade gossip, oh don't you know?

A crab in a tux, so dapper and bright,
Sashays in style, with sheer delight.
He checks his watch, 'I'm late for a meal!'
And scuttles away, with a flip and a wheel.

Octopuses wear hats, quite over the top,
With colors that change, they never do stop.
They tickle the corals while playing their game,
Making us giggle, 'What's in a name?'

For down beneath, there's laughter and cheer,
In the watery world, where life's held dear.
So let's dive deep, leave worries at bay,
Where silliness reigns, and fish dance all day.

Ballad of the Coral Depths

In the coral's embrace, where colors collide,
Fish flit and flutter, in whimsical stride.
A parrotfish squawks, 'I'm Picasso today!'
While a shy clownfish hides, in a peek-a-boo play.

Stars of the ocean, with swagger they swim,
Corals giggle as they frolic on whim.
A lionfish prances, all spiky and bold,
'Can I join this dance?' he bravely has told.

But oh dear jelly, with a bounce and a flip,
Needs to remember, it's not a boat trip!
In every sweep, there's a tale to recount,
From the depths of the coral, where laughter canount.

As they swirl and twirl, in a colorful craze,
Creatures unite with their vibrant displays.
Within this embrace, joy never descends,
For the ballad of life, here always transcends.

The Ocean's Breath at Dawn

As waves awake with yawns of foam,
They tickle toes, a water poem.
Seagulls squawk, what a silly crew,
They can't decide—dive or brew?

The sun peeks in, a golden grin,
Dancing on the waves, let the fun begin!
Fish flip-flop, a slippery show,
I think they're playing, don't you know?

A crab in costume, walking by,
Dressed in shells, oh me, oh my!
He waves a claw, but can't quite stand,
Perhaps he dreams of a marching band?

So here we stand, with laughter loud,
At dawn's fair stage, a playful crowd.
With whispers soft from tossing tides,
We're all just kids, caught in the rides.

Soft Embrace of Solitude

Alone on the shore, I take a seat,
The waves tell jokes, oh so discreet.
A dolphin's laugh, a splashy jest,
How many fish can swim like the best?

A starfish waves, it's quite the star,
But rolling sand is where we are.
They chat about currents, gossip of sand,
While I just sit, with drink in hand.

A crabby friend, all grumpy and pouty,
Complains of surfers, oh, so shouty.
But here on my towel, with sunblock thick,
I chuckle at life, it's quite the trick!

With whispers shared, the ocean grins,
In solitude, my laughter spins.
A sandcastle falls, oh what a scene,
Life's comedic flow, like a circuit machine.

Murmured Secrets of the Shoreline

The tide tells secrets with a splash,
As seashells giggle, in a bash.
They whisper tales of salty fun,
Of crabs who dance and fish who run.

A jellyfish wobbles in the glow,
With dangling arms, it puts on a show.
But watch your toes, the seaweed's sly,
It'll grab you fast, oh my, oh my!

Funny fish play hide and seek,
While gulls steal fries—their main technique.
With sandy jokes that never end,
The shoreline's laughter is my best friend.

As wind tickles waves with a cheeky grin,
I toss in woes and take the win.
The ocean sings, and I cannot hide,
In this watery world, I take my ride.

A Caress of Aqua Hues

What color is water, a bright turquoise?
Or just a splash from a boat's loud noise?
It swirls and twirls, a dance of cheer,
Inviting all in for a puddle clear.

The sun joins in with jolly rays,
While surfers laugh in their slippery ways.
A fish with shades swims by in style,
I think it's searching for a friendly smile.

Pastries and beach balls float in the tide,
As seagulls argue and we seek to hide.
The ocean quips, "Come in and play!"
My towel laughs: "You'll regret it today!"

Each wave's soft touch tells tales of mirth,
In aqua hues, we find rebirth.
Summer's delight wrapped in giggles and breezes,
With each splash and ripple, the joy never ceases.

Secrets in the Surf's Embrace

A fish wore a hat, quite dapper and neat,
Telling tales of the ocean, oh what a treat!
With each splash and giggle, waves joined the chorus,
Making dolphins chuckle, quite wondrous and porous.

Jellyfish dancing, in ballet so grand,
Twisting and twirling, they drew quite a band.
Seaweed chimed in, with a swaying groove,
As crabs brought the rhythm, their pinchers to move.

Seagulls debated while perched on a rock,
Who could spot snacks, those crafty sea hawks?
One flapped and flailed, but plopped with a thud,
Leaving friends in stitches, as he landed in mud.

So next time you hear, the ocean's soft call,
Remember those antics, the laughter of all.
Hidden treasures lie where the waves meet the sun,
In secrets we share, we find joy and fun.

Caressing Waves of Solitude

A crab in a tux, quite ready to dance,
Takes a bow on the sand, giving romance a chance.
With a wink at a starfish, all glimmering bright,
They twirled on the shoreline, a whimsical sight.

Gentle tides giggled, teasing shells on the shore,
Making snails blush, as they raced back for more.
One slippery eel, with a slick little grin,
Thought he was winning, but fell in the din.

Seashells were gossiping, sharing their lore,
Telling tales of sailors who landed before.
With each swaying ripple, another tale spun,
Time flies on the waves, but the fun's just begun.

So if you feel lonely, just listen and see,
The antics of mariners, and crabs having glee.
Among the soft shadows, where laughter does swell,
Every wave holds a secret, a tale meant to tell.

Soft Currents of Reflection

One wise old turtle wore glasses so thick,
Claimed he could read, with a flick and a click.
Mussels all nodded, with shells shining bright,
While fish wove around, in a fin-tastic flight.

The tide pooled its laughter, just like a jest,
While a seal made a face, putting humor to test.
He rolled on his back, with a belly so round,
Making waves ripple, such joy could be found.

A pelican pondered, on finding his lunch,
Missed by a krill in a slippery crunch.
With a flurry of feathers, he missed just by luck,
While clams cheered him on from their homes with a cluck.

So ponder not deeply, if laughter seems thin,
Just dive in the currents, and let joy begin.
For not all reflections are serious at sea,
Some bring out the giggles, eternally free.

Conversations with the Water's Edge

A shore crab exclaimed, "What's with all the fuss?"
As waves debated, creating a bus.
"Is it just me, or are waves getting bold?
They're splashing and laughing, like stories retold!"

A friendly old otter, with a slick, furry pelt,
Said, "Life's too short to be stubborn or dealt!"
So they juggled sea cucumbers, all wriggly and weird,
While starfish all cheered, as laughter appeared.

The breeze, it chimed in, with a whisper so sly,
"Let's play hide-and-seek, under cotton candy skies!"
Fish darted and danced, in swift, sneaky swirls,
As crabs counted loudly, "One…two… here come the pearls!"

So gather your giggles, at the water's nice edge,
Where fun takes a swim, and worries can hedge.
Every splash is a story, each ripple a laugh,
In playful convos where nature finds craft.

Dreams Adrift on Gentle Currents

A clam with style in a shell so bright,
He dances the cha-cha, what a funny sight!
Jellyfish float, they can't really swim,
Waving their arms, looking quite grim.

The seagulls squawk in a comical spree,
Stealing my fries, as happy as can be!
Stars on the water do a twinkling swirl,
While fish throw a party, giving a twirl.

Conversations with the Horizon

The sun winks down with a golden grin,
While crabs have gossip, stirring their kin.
A turtle shuffles, slow but aware,
Of fish in tuxedos who vanish mid-air.

Ping-ponging waves have a playful chat,
As dolphins giggle, saying, "Look at that!"
Seashells giggle, in whispers so sly,
Thinking of moments to wave goodbye.

Reflections in the Quiet Tide

A starfish on the sand, still as a rock,
Dreams of a dance with a clock-watching sock.
Mermaids chuckle, their tails in a twist,
Claiming the beach was on their wish list.

Octopuses juggle with crabs in the storm,
Creating a circus, it's their favorite norm.
Waves make a splash, they say, 'We're the tide!'
With sandcastles booming, they're filled up with pride.

Hushed Waves at Dusk

A boat shaped like broccoli drifts down below,
With fish in a band playing music, you know.
Napping otters snore like an old grandpa,
While gulls wear sunglasses, quite the flair-a!

The moon peeks out with a goofy grin,
As crabs breakdance, inviting their kin.
Whispers of laughter create a soft night,
As gurgling giggles fade into twilight.

A Soft Caress on Sandy Shores

A crab in a bowtie danced with glee,
While seagulls squawked their comedy.
Shells wore glasses, oh what a sight,
As waves tickled toes, pure delight.

Sunbathers laughed with melon hats,
Chasing after sneaky, beachy mats.
Sandcastles tumbled, a royal mess,
To the tide's laughter, we all confess.

Fish in tuxedos swam with flair,
While dolphins flipped without a care.
A jellyfish floated like a queen,
In the splashy ocean, a funny scene.

So here's to the antics, wild and free,
A summer ride, just you and me.
With a wink from the waves, we'll play forever,
In laughter and silliness, oh, what a treasure!

Murmurs of the Tidal Moon

The moon slipped on a silky wave,
Whispered secrets that couldn't behave.
Starfish wore crowns, aiming for fame,
While crabs staged a play, calling your name.

A whale with a mustache sang a tune,
While fish dressed up for a fancy swoon.
Mermaids danced, tails all aglow,
As ocean currents laughed a sweet "whoa!"

With tidal waves making jokes so grand,
A humor-filled tide mapped out the land.
Surfboards giggled on waves of foam,
Who knew the ocean could feel like home?

So, let's ride the ripples where giggles reside,
In this watery realm, let's take a ride.
With every splash, a chuckle combined,
In the moonlight's rhythm, laughter we find.

Infinite Calm of Aquatic Dreams

In a bubble bath of playful tides,
Fish read stories where laughter hides.
An octopus juggled pearls with zest,
As sea turtles wore vests for a quest.

A starry-eyed clam played hide and seek,
While barnacles giggled, their humor unique.
Splashing and frolicking far and wide,
In this busy ocean, all can abide.

Sandy mermaids with hair of kelp,
Told jokes of whales that made us yelp.
The corals chuckled, colors so bright,
Creating a jest with each beam of light.

So drift in these currents, so lively and free,
With echoes of laughter as vast as the sea.
In the depths of the waters, joy swims around,
Where funny fish tales in abundance abound.

Breath of the Ocean's Dreams

Waves frolicked on shores, a playful dance,
While gulls were dressed for a fancy chance.
Anemones laughed as they tickled the sand,
The ocean's breath, a whimsical band.

A hippo in swim trunks dove with a splash,
While crabs wore shades—quite the fashion flash!
Seashells clinked like glasses raised high,
In a toast to the tides, they waved goodbye.

Dolphins flipped in synchronized cheer,
While jellybeans popped up, oh dear!
With every swell, a giggle we made,
In this bath of giggles, we never fade.

So let humor flow on this bright sunny shore,
Where laughter and waves forever explore.
In the breath of the depths, let's laugh till we drop,
For the ocean's wild spirit will never stop!

Gentle Hand of the Tide

The waves tickle toes, what a funny prank,
They pull back in laughter, oh, what a tank!
Seagulls squawk jokes from their lofty height,
While crabs dance a shuffle, an odd little sight.

With each playful splash, a giggle erupts,
As beach balls soar high, then land with a thud.
Sandcastles might crumble, but who really cares?
The tide rolls in, smiling, it's all in the airs.

Kids chase after shells like they're treasure rare,
While fish swim by, giggling with flair.
"A splashy affair!" the dolphins do sing,
As waves play a tune on the mermaid's bling.

So join in the fun, let your worries float,
Embrace the whimsy, let laughter emote!
For in the ocean's play, we all find our glee,
In the gentle hand of this watery spree.

The Soft Embrace of the Deep

Bubbles rise up like giggles of fish,
Dreaming of candy in a jelly-twist swish.
Octopus jokes with its wiggly arms,
While seaweed dances, its hair full of charms.

A turtle told me, in a voice quite sage,
"Take life slow—be the star of your stage!"
But then it tripped over its own shell's weight,
And rolled off, still laughing—oh, isn't fate great?

Seashells are calendars, hailed by the tide,
Each one holds a secret, a story, a ride.
In marshmallow clouds of fluffy white foam,
The ocean's soft whispers call everyone home.

The jellyfish, glowing, throws a small bash,
While crabs pull pranks that make all of us laugh.
With each silky wave, humor sweeps shore to shore,
Tucked deep in the heart of the ocean's soft core.

Nestled in the Ocean's Lap

Oh, how snug it feels, in this watery bed,
With starfish doing yoga, their flippers outspread.
Clams open wide, with a wink and a smile,
"Come join us for lunch, it's a fun little trial!"

A dolphin zips past, with a whoop and a dive,
Chasing a bubble, feeling so alive.
While sea turtles giggle, their feet in a race,
Saying, "We take it slow; it's not a mad pace!"

The colors of coral dance in delight,
Like a party where every shade shines so bright.
With laughter of waves, and jokes from the tide,
We all are just kids, in this ocean wide.

So here in the swell, let us frolic and play,
Nestled close together, chasing cares away.
For in this blue cradle, life's humor runs free,
In the joyful embrace of the deep's gentle spree.

Echoes of the Salty Breeze

The breeze carries tales, of fish in disguise,
Blowing laughter like bubbles 'neath bright sunny skies.
Whales tell us secrets, but only on night's cue,
While starfish all giggle at how much we construe.

Seagulls swoop down, and they steal a french fry,
Making faces so silly, you just can't deny.
"Come join us!" they chortle with feathers all fluffed,
As the ocean's soft whispers keep telling us 'tough.'

A crab wears a hat, made of seaweed and sand,
Declaring it fashion, its new style is grand.
With every swell, oh! The sea chuckles bright,
As laughter erupts, echoing through the night.

So listen, dear friends, to the ocean's giggle,
Feel the breeze dance, and the tides play their riddle.
For life's just a joke, and we're all in the skit,
In this funny drift, let's never forget!

The Sound of Tranquil Currents

A fish wore a hat, thought he was quite cool,
He danced with the waves, like a fishy fool.
Seagulls squawked loudly, took his fame,
They stole his snacks, oh, what a shame!

A crab on a rock, flipping through the news,
Wavy-eyed, he mused, in his old rubber shoes.
Turtles played chess, checking with glee,
While starfish just stared, sipping iced tea.

A dolphin arrived, threw a fish to the crowd,
The octopus clapped, feeling ever so proud.
With splashes and gurgles, they partied all night,
Until jellyfish glowed, oh, what a sight!

So here by the shore, let the laughter ignite,
With fishy tomfoolery, our spirits take flight.
No worries or woes in this watery space,
Just fun by the currents, a joy to embrace.

Nighttime Lull in the Tide

As the moon took a dip, the crabs all conspired,
To build a big castle, they were quite inspired.
Clams brought the snacks, oysters played tunes,
While dolphins jumped high, waving goodbyes to the moons.

The tide laughed so hard, it nearly fell over,
As a clam told a joke, oh, wasn't it clever?
The fish swam around in circles they spun,
While the tide hummed a lullaby, just for fun.

A starfish snored loudly, stole all the scene,
As a crab tiptoed softly, feeling quite keen.
"What's this night farce?" said a snooty old seal,
"I'd rather be fishing, it's the real deal!"

Yet here on the shore, under starlit delight,
The crabs held their feast, giggling through the night.
With bubbles of laughter that twinkled like stars,
Nighttime's sweet frolic was truly bizarre.

Poetics of Water's Edge

A rubber duck floated, quite bold and so bright,
He threw parties for plankton till late in the night.
With waves as his dancers, they formed a dance team,
While seaweed waved proudly, living the dream.

An octopus crooned, with eight arms to play,
His karaoke night made everyone sway.
With fish in the crowd, they belted out tunes,
While sea turtles laughed, munching on prunes.

Sandcastles stood tall, till a wave said "Hello!"
But they laughed and they danced, for they knew it was show.
Each grain of sand chimed, in unison, bold,
As laughter and joy in the water took hold.

At the edge of the world, the silliness grew,
With bubbles of giggles rising up to the blue.
So come to the shore, leave worries behind,
In the symphony of laughter, let joy be defined.

A Symphony of Ocean Breezes

A whale in a tux looked dapper and fine,
He waltzed with a clam, and they drew quite a line.
Their dance was a sight, with fins flapping wide,
While shrimp threw confetti, full of pride.

Seagulls were staging a stand-up routine,
Cracking up fish with humor unseen.
A crab told a joke, made jellyfish laugh,
As waves swirled around, they were not quite daft.

The moon lit the water, a spotlight so grand,
While sea stars applauded, taking a stand.
A party erupted from dusk until dawn,
As sea foam performed a bubbly ballet on.

With laughter and cheer, the salt air did sing,
Together they danced, in a shimmering ring.
In this wacky sea world, oh, what a delight,
Where breezes of fun turned the dull into bright!

Ocean's Soft Serenade

Waves giggle as they crash,
Fish dance in a splash.
Seagulls squawk a silly tune,
While crabs do the cha-cha at noon.

Sandy toes and sunburned noses,
Jellyfish wear fancy poses.
A soft breeze gives a poke,
Just watch out for that seaweed cloak!

Sandcastles come with moats so grand,
Built by a not-so-great hand.
They tumble down with quite a thud,
All that's left is a dopey stud!

Seashells chime like silver bells,
While dolphins share their silly quells.
Stars come out with a twinkle and flip,
The ocean's jokes give your heart a skip.

Murmurs of the Tidal Breeze

Crabs wear hats, a sight to behold,
With stories of humor yet untold.
The water's lapping sings with glee,
As fish propose a grass dance spree.

Salty air fills up with laughs,
Octopuses share their goofy halves.
A buoy bobs like a big ol' clown,
Making waves as it bounces down.

Seagulls steal fries, oh what a fuss,
Surfers stumble, laugh, and cuss.
With each wave, the fun cascades,
As beach umbrellas do wild charades!

Tide pools giggle with a splash,
Bubbles pop in a not-so-quiet crash.
The ocean whispers, "Let's play a game,"
"Make sure to join in on the fame!"

Lullabies of the Aquatic Depths

Bubbles rise like tiny balloons,
Fish are hosting wild festoons.
Shells clap along with the fun,
As eels take turns in the run.

Barnacles wear silly socks,
While dolphins jump like happy clocks.
A playful wave nudges with cheer,
"Come join us, the party's right here!"

Starfish making silly faces,
Crab races fill all the spaces.
With so much joy, it's hard to miss,
Underwater pranks sealed with a kiss.

Mollusks giggle in their shell beds,
Waking up with topped-up spreads.
As the sun sets, they whisper low,
"Who knew the depths could steal the show?"

Embrace of the Salty Winds

The breeze teases your hair just so,
As waves perform a funny show.
Seagulls compete in a silly race,
While starfish wink with a goofy face.

Turtles in shades, what a sight!
Surfboards wobbling left and right.
With every swell, a laugh ignites,
As goofy antics fill the nights.

Popcorn shrimp toss a theater play,
Crabs practice their ballet display.
The ocean waves hold stories grand,
Of joy and laughter across the sand.

Winds howl jokes from far and near,
Seashells chuckle as you draw near.
Under the stars, the giggles blend,
In this salty world, laughter's the trend!